CALLING

A

WOLF

A

WOLF

CALLING

A

WOLF

A

WOLF

poems by

Kaveh Akbar

ALICE JAMES BOOKS
FARMINGTON, MAINE
www.alicejamesbooks.org

10 9 8 7 6 5 4

Alice James Books are published by Alice James Poetry Cooperative, Inc.,
an affiliate of the University of Maine at Farmington.

Alice James Books
114 Prescott Street
Farmington, ME 04938
www.alicejamesbooks.org

Library of Congress Cataloging-in-Publication Data

Names: Akbar, Kaveh. author.
Title: Calling a wolf a wolf / Kaveh Akbar.
Description: Farmington, Maine : Alice James Books, 2017.
Identifiers: LCCN 2017015979 (print) | LCCN 2017028090 (ebook) | ISBN
    9781938584725 (eBook) | ISBN 9781938584671 (paperback)
Subjects: LCSH: Alcoholism--Poetry. | Alcoholics--Rehabilitation--Poetry. |
    Poetry. | BISAC: POETRY / American / General. | POETRY / Middle Eastern. |
    POETRY / Inspirational & Religious.
Classification: LCC PS3601.A43 (ebook) | LCC PS3601.A43 .A6 2017 (print) |
    DDC 811/.6--dc23
LC record available at https://lccn.loc.gov/2017015979

Alice James Books gratefully acknowledges support from individual donors, private foun-
dations, the University of Maine at Farmington, the National
Endowment for the Arts, and the Amazon Literary Partnership.

ART WORKS. arts.gov   amazon *literary partnership*

Contributions for this reprint were made by The Frank M. Barnard Foundation.

Cover art: "Il Digiuno" by Nicola Samori / 2014 / Oil on copper / 100 x 100 cm
/ Courtesy Galerie EIGEN + ART

CONTENTS

III. Irons

ACKNOWLEDGMENTS

A great debt of gratitude is owed to the editors of the following publications where these poems first appeared, often in earlier versions:

The Adroit Journal: "Calling a Wolf a Wolf (Inpatient)"
AGNI: "God"
American Poetry Review: "Being in This World Makes Me Feel Like a Time Traveler," "Best Shadows," "Exciting the Canvas"
At Length: "Drinkaware Self-Report"
Bennington Review: "Wild Pear Tree," "Desunt Nonnulla,"
Black Warrior Review: "I Won't Lie This Plague of Gratitude"
BOAAT: "Neither Now nor Never"
Boston Review: "Portrait of the Alcoholic with Craving"
Copper Nickel: "Portrait of the Alcoholic with Doubt and Kingfisher"
Crab Orchard Review: "Wake Me Up When It's My Birthday"
Denver Quarterly: "Thirstiness Is Not Equal Division," "Portrait of the Alcoholic Frozen in Block of Ice"
Diagram: "So Often the Body Becomes a Distraction"
Diode: "Portrait of the Alcoholic with Withdrawal"
FIELD: "What Seems Like Joy"
Guernica: "Tassiopeia"
Gulf Coast: "Fugu"
Harvard Divinity Bulletin: "Soot"
Hayden's Ferry Review: "Personal Inventory: Fearless (Temporis Fila)"
Indiana Review: "Portrait of the Alcoholic with Home Invader and Housefly"
The Journal: "Orchids Are Sprouting from the Floorboards"
jubilat: "Besides, Little Goat, You Can't Just Go Asking for Mercy"
The Literary Review: "Everything That Moves Is Alive and a Threat—a Reminder"
Lit Hub: "Long Pig"
The Los Angeles Review: "Portrait of the Alcoholic Stranded Alone on a Desert Island"
Muzzle: "Supplication with Rabbit Skull and Bouquet"
Narrative: "Do You Speak Persian?"
Nashville Review: "Portrait of the Alcoholic Three Weeks Sober"

New England Review: "No Is a Complete Sentence"
The New Yorker: "What Use Is Knowing Anything if No One Is Around"
The Offing: "Palmyra"
PANK: "The Straw Is Too Long, the Axe Is Too Dull"
Ploughshares: "Yeki Bood, Yeki Nabood," "Ways to Harm a Thing"
Poetry: "Portrait of the Alcoholic Floating in Space with Severed Umbilicus,"
     "River of Milk," "My Kingdom for a Murmur of Fanfare"
Poetry Society of America: "Heritage"
Puerto del Sol: "Some Boys Aren't Born They Bubble"
Redivider: "Prayer"
Sixth Finch: "Stop Me If You've Heard This One Before"
Sonora Review: "Despite Their Size Children Are Easy to Remember They
     Watch You"
Spoon River Poetry Review: "Milk"
THRUSH: "Portrait of the Alcoholic with Moths and River"
Tin House: "Every Drunk Wants to Die Sober It's How We Beat the Game,"
     "Against Dying," "Against Hell"
TriQuarterly: "Unburnable the Cold is Flooding Our Lives"
Vinyl Poetry: "Rimrock"
Virginia Quarterly Review: "The New World," "A Boy Steps into the Water"
Waxwing: "Learning to Pray," "Recovery"
West Branch: "An Apology"
ZYZZYVA: "Portrait of the Alcoholic with Relapse Fantasy"

Portrait of the Alcoholic, a short chapbook containing several of these poems, was published by Sibling Rivalry Press in January 2017.

"Fugu" was anthologized in *Best New Poets 2016*.
"Portrait of the Alcoholic with Relapse Fantasy" was selected to be reprinted in
     Pushcart Prize XLII: Best of the Small Presses.
"Neither Now Nor Never" was anthologized in *The Orison Anthology 2016*.
"Palmyra" was reprinted for *PBS NewsHour*.
"Heritage" was awarded the Lucille Medwick Memorial Prize by the Poetry
     Society of America.

Deep abiding gratitude to Chris Forhan, Alessandra Lynch, Steve Henn, David J. Thompson, Carey Salerno, Bryan Borland, Seth Pennington, Don Share, francine j. harris, Eduardo C. Corral, Frank Bidart, Fanny Howe, Max Ritvo, Aimee Nezhukumatathil, Gabrielle Calvocoressi, Arash Saedinia, Ruth Baumann, James Kimbrell, David Kirby, Jayme Ringleb, Rosebud Ben-Oni, Martha Rhodes, Robert Olen Butler, Kelly Butler, Solmaz Sharif, Yona Harvey, Kazim Ali, Nick Flynn, Jonathan Farmer, Sean Shearer, Gretchen Marquette, David Tomas Martinez, Zack Strait, Allison Wright, Ellen Bryant Voigt, Andrew Epstein, Damian Caudill, Chase Noelle, Carl Phillips, Alyssa Graffam, Darrian Church, Julia Bouwsma, Tomaž Šalamun, Michael Purol, Thaddeus Harmon, Wanda, Mammy, Arash, Mytoan, Nora, and Layla for their patience and love and support.

My thanks to Franz Wright, Reyhaneh Jabbari, W.H. Auden, Ali Akbar Sadeghi, Khaled al-Asaad, Carolus Linnæus, Aaron Weiss, Fanny Howe, Sohrab Sepehri, Lydia Henn, Leslie Jamison, Diane Seuss, Gertrude Stein, Kahlil Gibran, Max Ritvo, Dan Barden, and all other voices in the choir.

An eternity of wild love and gratitude to Paige Lewis, who all this is meant to impress.

for Dan

SOOT

Sometimes God comes to earth disguised as rust,
chewing away a chain link fence or mariner's knife.
From up so close we must seem
clumsy and gloomless, like new lovers

undressing in front of each other
for the first time. Regarding loss, I'm afraid
to keep it in the story,
worried what I might bring back to life,

like the marble angel who woke to find
his innards scattered around his feet.
Blood from the belly tastes sweeter
than blood from anywhere else. We know this

but don't know why—the woman on TV
dabs a man's gutwound with her hijab
then draws the cloth to her lips, confused.
I keep dreaming I'm a creature pulling out my claws

one by one to sell in a market stall next to stacks
of pomegranates and garden tools. It's predictable,
the logic of dreams. Long ago I lived in Heaven
because I wanted to. When I fell to earth

I knew the way—through the soot, into the leaves.
It still took years. Upon landing, the ground
embraced me sadly, with the gentleness
of someone delivering tragic news to a child.

I. TERMINAL

"All sins tend to be addictive, and the terminal point
of addiction is damnation."

—W. H. AUDEN

WILD PEAR TREE

it's been January for months in both directions   frost
over grass like pale fungus like
mothdust   the branches of the pear tree are pickling
in ice white as the long white line running from me
to the smooth whales frozen in chunks of ocean
from their vast bobbing to the blackwhite
stars flowering into heaven   the hungry cat gnaws
on a sliver of mirror and I have been chewing
out my stitches wondering which
warm names we should try singing
wild thyme cowslip blacksnake   all the days
in a year line up at the door and I deflect each saying *no*
you will not be needed one by one they skulk off
into the cold   the cat hates this place more than he loves
me he cannot remember the spring when I fed him
warm duck fat daily nor the kitchen vase filled with musky blue
roses nor the pear tree which was so eager to toss its fruit so sweet
it made us sleepy   I stacked the pears on the mantle
until I ran out of room and began filling them into
the bathtub   one evening I slid in as if into a mound
of jewels   now ghost finches leave footprints
on our snowy windowsills   the cat paces
through the night listening for their chirps   our memories
have frosted over   ages ago we guzzled
all the rosewater in the vase still we check for it
nightly   I have forgotten even
the easy prayer I was supposed to use
in emergencies   something something I was not
born here I was not born here I was not

DO YOU SPEAK PERSIAN?

Some days we can see Venus in midafternoon. Then at night, stars
separated by billions of miles, light traveling years

to die in the back of an eye.

Is there a vocabulary for this—one to make dailiness amplify
and not diminish wonder?

I have been so careless with the words I already have.

I don't remember how to say *home*
in my first language, or *lonely*, or *light*.

I remember only
delam barat tang shodeh, I miss you,

and *shab bekheir*, good night.

How is school going, Kaveh-joon?
Delam barat tang shodeh.

Are you still drinking?
Shab bekheir.

For so long every step I've taken
has been from one tongue to another.

To order the world:
I need, you need, he/she/it needs.

The rest, left to a hungry jackal
in the back of my brain.

Right now our moon looks like a pale cabbage rose.
Delam barat tang shodeh.

We are forever folding into the night.
Shab bekheir.

YEKI BOOD YEKI NABOOD

every day someone finds what they need
in someone else
                           you tear into a body
and come out with a fistful of the exact
feathers you were looking for wondering
why anyone would want to swallow
so many perfect feathers
                                    everyone
looks uglier naked or at least
I do my pillar of fuzz my damp
lettuce
            I hoarded an entire decade
of bliss of brilliant dime-sized raptures
and this is what I have to show
for it a catastrophe of joints this
puddle I'm soaking in which came
from my crotch and never did
dry
        the need
to comfort anyone else to pull
the sickle from their chest seems
unsummonable now as a childhood
pet as Farsi or tears
                              I used to slow
dance with my mother in our living
room spiritless as any prince I felt
the bark of her spine softening I became
an agile brute she became a stuffed
ox I hear this happens
all over the world

PORTRAIT OF THE ALCOHOLIC WITH HOME INVADER AND HOUSEFLY

It felt larger than it was, the knife
that pushed through my cheek.

Immediately I began leaking:
blood and saliva, soft as smoke. I had been asleep,

safe from sad news, dreaming
of my irradiated hairless mother

pulling a thorn from the eye of a dog.
I woke from that into a blade. Everything

seemed cast in lapis and spinning light,
like an ancient frieze in Damascus.

Listen to me, faithful silence: somehow
we've become strangers. Growing up

I kept a housefly tied to a string tied to a lamp.
I fed him wet Tic Tacs and idly assumed

he would outlive me. When he died
I opened myself to death, the way a fallen tree

opens itself to the wild. Now my blood
is drying on the pillow. Now the man

who held the knife is gone, elsewhere
and undiminished. I can hardly remember

anything about him. It can be difficult
telling the size of something

when it's right above you—the average
cumulus cloud weighing as much

as eighty elephants. The things I've thought I've loved
could sink an ocean liner, and likely would

if given the chance. From my window,
the blinking windmills seem

further away than ever before. My beard
has matted itself into a bloody poultice,

and a woman's voice on TV is begging for charity.
She says *please* and reads a phone number. Soon I will

mumble a few words in Arabic to settle back
into sleep. If morning arrives, I will wash my face.

RECOVERY

First, setting down the glass.

Then the knives.

Black resin seeps

into the carpet.

According to science,

I should be dead.

Lyptus table, unsteady

boat, drifts away.

Angostura, agave,

elderflower, rye—

the whole paradisal

bouquet spins apart.

Here, I am graceless.

No. Worse than that.

DRINKAWARE SELF-REPORT

—How many drinks do you have per week?

I drink what I drink lie where I lie I
deserve all the things I desire   cocktail
chatter cymbals crashing green pills
which long ago stopped working
which I still carry to trade for
cigarettes or pitchers of Old Style it almost
feels like cheating

*—How often during the last year have you found that you were not able to
stop drinking once you had started?*

I am an ugly boy but it's a pretty
day everywhere hard blue snow and old
men arguing the facts of a story they
weren't even born for   they hate me I am
the only person here not grieving

*—How often during the last year have you had a feeling of guilt or remorse
after drinking?*

filthy with pride I am standing as ever before watch
me sing through the jaw of a mouse about
the old miracles   a crimson robe floating
up from the Gobi
                    sand into prophet then back into sand

*—How often during the last year have you been unable to recall what
happened the night before because you had been drinking?*

even the river is tired of its slimy brown water there is no end to
wanting   pensioners walk around a mall ogling
watches they'll never buy   one collapses
in front of the display case his skin
shimmers with sweat he looks
like a great carp

—Have you or somebody else been injured as a result of your drinking?

under gold

light my

hands look

gold I

long to

be aes-

theti-

cized

to have

my bones

laced with

silver

my eyes

blooming

into

marguerites

CALLING A WOLF A WOLF (INPATIENT)

like the sky I've been too quiet   everyone's forgotten I'm here   I've tried all
the usual tricks   pretending I've just been made terrifying   like a suddenly
carnivorous horse   like a rabid hissing sapphire   the medical response has
been clear   *sit patiently until invited to leave*   outside the lake is evaporat-
ing   dry blue like a galley proof   a month ago they dragged up a drowned
tourist   his bloatwhite belly filled with radishes and lamb shank   his
entire digestive system was a tiny museum of pleasure   compared to him I
am healthy and unremarkable   here I am reading a pharmaceutical brochure
here I am dying at an average pace   envy is the only deadly sin that's no fun
for the sinner   this makes sadness seem more like a tradition   loyalty to
a parent's past   I try to find small comforts   purple clover growing in the
long grass   a yellow spider on the windowsill   I am less horrible than I could
be   I've never set a house on fire   never thrown a firstborn off a bridge
still my whole life I answered every cry for help with a pour   with a turning
away   I've given this coldness many names   thinking if it had a name it
would have a solution   thinking if I called a wolf a wolf I might dull its fangs
I carried the coldness like a diamond for years   holding it close   near as
blood   until one day I woke and it was fully inside me   both of us ruined
and unrecognizable   two coins on a train track   the train crushed into one

STOP ME IF YOU'VE HEARD THIS ONE BEFORE

I can't even remember my name, I who remember
so much—football scores, magic tricks, deep love
so close to God it was practically religious.

When you fall asleep in that sort of love
you wake up with bruises on your neck. I don't
have drunks, sirs, I have adventures. Every day

my body follows me around asking
for things. I try to think louder, try
to be brilliant, wildly brilliant. We all want

the same thing (to walk in sincere wonder,
like the first man to hear a parrot speak), but we live
on an enormous flatness floating between

two oceans. Sometimes you just have to leave
whatever's real to you, you have to clomp
through fields and kick the caps off

all the toadstools. Sometimes
you have to march all the way to Galilee
or the literal foot of God himself before you realize

you've already passed the place where
you were supposed to die. I can no longer remember
the being afraid, only that it came to an end.

PORTRAIT OF THE ALCOHOLIC WITH WITHDRAWAL

everyone wants to know
      what I saw on the long walk
away from you

        I couldn't eat
    and didn't sleep
        for an entire week

I can hardly picture any of it now
      save the fox I thought
was in the grass but wasn't

        I remember him quiet
    as a telescope
        tiny as a Plutonian moon

everything else
      was wilding around us
the sky and the wind

        the riptides and
    the rogue comet
        blasting toward earth

do you remember this
      I introduced myself
by one of the names

        I kept back then
    the fox was so still
        I could have called him anything

SOME BOYS AREN'T BORN THEY BUBBLE

some boys aren't born they bubble
      up from the earth's crust   land safely around
kitchen tables green globes of fruit already

        in their mouths   when they find themselves crying
     they stop crying these boys moan
        more than other boys   they do as desire

demands   when they dance their bodies plunge
      into space and recover   the music stays
in their breastbones they sing songs about

       storms then dry their shoes on porches
    these boys are so cold their pilot lights never light
       they buy the best heat money can buy   blue flames

swamp smoke   they are desperate
     to lick and be licked   sometimes one will eat
all the food in a house or break every bone

       in his jaw   sometimes one will disappear into himself
    like a ram charging a mirror when this happens
       they all feel it   afterwards the others dream

of rain their pupils boil they light black candles
     and pray the only prayer they know   *oh lord*
spare this body   set fire to another

HERITAGE

*Reyhaneh Jabbari, a twenty-six-year-old Iranian woman, was hanged
on October 25ᵗʰ, 2014 for killing a man who was attempting to rape her.*

the body is a mosque borrowed from Heaven   centuries of time
stain the glazed brick   our skin rubs away like a chip
in the middle of an hourglass   sometimes I am so ashamed

of my sentience how little it matters   angels don't care about humility
you shaved your head   spent eleven days half-starved in solitary
and not a single divine trumpet wept into song   now it's lonely all over

I'm becoming more a vessel of memories than a person   it's a myth
that love lives in the heart   it lives in the throat we push it out
when we speak   when we gasp we take a little for ourselves

in books love can be war-ending   a soldier drops his sword
to lie forking oysters into his enemy's mouth   in life we hold love up to the light
to marvel at its impotence   you said in a letter to Sholeh

you weren't even killing the roaches in your cell   that you would take them up
by their antennae and flick them through the bars into a courtyard
where you could see men hammering long planks of cypress into gallows

the same men who years before threw their rings in the mud   who watered them
five times daily   who shot blackbirds off almond branches
and kissed the soil at the sight of sprouts   then cursed each other when the stalks

which should have licked their lips withered dryly at their knees   may God beat
us awake   scourge our brains to life   may we measure every victory
by the momentary absence of pain   there is no solace in history   this is a gift

we are given at birth   a pocket we fold into at death   goodbye now you mountain
you armada of flowers   you entire miserable decade in a lump in my throat
despite all our endlessly rehearsed rituals of mercy   it was you we sent on

MILK

the geese are curving around the horizon drawing maps
a curve is a straight line broken at all its points so much
of being alive is breaking
                              the indestructible red beetles
are growing weaker they no longer delight in their collecting
bark bits of tobacco a chip of goat bone   would you rather
have a day begin in silence and end in song or the opposite you
can't have both   once I went silent for a week once I couldn't

walk for two months I lay in bed eating drugs   rocking
into paleness even the bright flurry of finches outside dull I worry
sometimes there is no true wildness
                              I cannot be trusted to return
what I've been given I need to be taken care of   paradise lies
at the feet of mothers I will believe you when you tell me your dreams
please mother me kiss all my secret rashes I am awake and will be

PORTRAIT OF THE ALCOHOLIC WITH DOUBT AND KINGFISHER

You just don't know yet which parts
           of yourself to value—
your spittle or its syrupy smell,

                    your irises or their mothish obsession
              with light. Even the trap-caught fox
                    knew enough to chew away its leg,

delighting (if such a thing can be said)
           at the relative softness of marrow.
Nature rewards this kind of courage—

                    a kingfisher shoots into a pond
              and comes out with a stickleback.
                    Starving mice will often eat their own tails

before ceding to hunger. The lesson:
           it's never too late to become
a new thing, to rip the fur

                    from your face and dive
              dimplefirst into the strange.
                    Some people don't even want to drink,

aren't tempted by the pools of liquor
           all around them. This seems
a selfishness. God loves the hungry

                    more than the full. Faith is a story
              about people totally unlike you
                    building concrete walls around their beds.

Behind each of their faces: a slowly dying
        animal. Do you feel summoned?
Do you feel heaven closing itself

             to you like a clamshell snapping shut?
        Blessed are those who can distract themselves
            and blessed are the distractions: a fuzzy purse

of bellyfat, a bit of mint growing wild
        along a driveway, china plates piled high with food
so pale you pepper it just to see it's there.

DESUNT NONNULLA

as a child I wasn't so much foreign as I was very small   my soul
still unsmogged by its station   I walked learning
the names of things each new title a tiny seizure
of joy   *paleontologist tarpaper marshmallow*   I polished them like trophies
eager in delight and color-blind   though I still loved crayons
for their names *cerulean gunmetal* and *corn-*
flower more than making up for the hues I couldn't tell apart   even
our great-grandparents saw different blues owing
to the rapid evolution of rods and cones   now I resist
acknowledging the riches I've inherited   hard bones and a mind full
of names   it's so much easier to catalog hunger to atomize
absence and carry each bit like ants taking home a meal

I am insatiable   every grievance levied against me
amounts to ingratitude   I need to be broken like an unruly mustang
like bitten skin   supposedly people hymned before names   their mouths
were zeroes little pleasure portals for taking in grape
leaves cloudberries the fingers of lovers   today words fly
in all directions   I don't know how anyone does
anything   I miss my mouth sipping coffee and spend
the day explaining the dribble to strangers who patiently
endure my argle-bargle before returning
to their appetites   I am not a slow learner   I am a quick forgetter
such erasing makes one voracious   if you teach me something
beautiful   I will name it quickly before it floats away

LEARNING TO PRAY

My father moved patiently
cupping his hands beneath his chin,
        kneeling on a janamaz

             then pressing his forehead to a circle
                of Karbala clay. Occasionally
             he'd glance over at my clumsy mirroring,

    my too-big Packers T-shirt
and pebble-red shorts,
        and smile a little, despite himself.

             Bending there with his whole form
                marbled in light, he looked like
             a photograph of a famous ghost.

    I ached to be so beautiful.
I hardly knew anything yet—
        not the boiling point of water

             or the capital of Iran,
                not the five pillars of Islam
             or the Verse of the Sword—

    I knew only that I wanted
to be like him,
        that twilit stripe of father

             mesmerizing as the bluewhite Iznik tile
                hanging in our kitchen, worshipped
             as the long faultless tongue of God.

PORTRAIT OF THE ALCOHOLIC THREE WEEKS SOBER

The first thing I ever saw die—a lamb that took ten
long minutes. Instead of rolling into the grass, her blood
pooled on the porch. My uncle stepped away
from the puddle, called it *a good omen for the tomatoes*
then lit a tiny black cigar. Years later I am still picking romas

out of my salads. The barbarism of eating anything
seems almost unbearable. With drinking however
I've always been prodigious. A garden bucket filled with cream
would disappear, and seconds later I'd emerge
patting my belly. I swear, I could conjure rain clouds

from piles of ash, guzzle down whole human bodies,
the faces like goblets I'd drain then put back in the cupboard.
So trust me now: when I say *thirst*, I mean defeated,
abandoned-in-faith, lonely-as-the-slow-charge-into-a-bayonet
thirst. Imagine being the sand forced to watch silt dance

in the Nile. Imagine being the oil boiling away an entire person.
Today, I'm finding problems in areas where I didn't have areas before.
I'm grateful to be trusted with any of it: the bluebrown ocean
undrinkable as a glass of scorpions, the omnipresent fragrant
honey and the bees that guard it. It just seems such a severe sort of

miraculousness. Even the terminal dryness of bone hides inside our skin
plainly, like dust on a mirror. This can guide us forward
or not guide us at all. Maybe it's that *forward* seems too chronological,
the way the future-perfect always sounds so cavalier
when someone tells me *some day this will all have been worth it.*

SUPPLICATION WITH RABBIT SKULL AND BOUQUET

take me by the elbow

can you see the bones left in my ear

our messiahs are blowing us kisses from heaven

they speak in the continental longhand

the doubt between us hangs like a moon

there is no such thing as certainty

the spell cast in the night was just a hard wind

your cup is still full of poison

whose blood is this on the bedsheets

not that cross

I'm thankful for your beaded carapace

I am a grown man

excuse the buttery light haloing my head

I lack money

can you help me with any of this

you have swallowed so much already

the fire under my bed is quiet as a fossil

I trust completely whatever's in your body

visit me at home where ghosts will watch us from the closet

take me by force

can you see the boy's name cut in my bark

our messiahs are hopeless and modern

they speak only in our sleep

the doubt between us stickies our tongues

there is no such thing as sorcery

the spell cast on your cup was just a heap of words

your cup was never there at all

whose blood is this on the cross

not any cross you know

I'm thankful for your yellow pills

I am growing into my science

excuse the rabbit skull crunching in my teeth

I lack sexual preference

can you help me shrink back to a dainty mouthful

you have swallowed even my bouquet of corn and straw

the fire under my bed is simple as a bed

I trust completely whatever's in your pockets

visit me at home and pin your money to my skin

EXCITING THE CANVAS

That the moon causes tides
seems too witchy to be science.
The sea purging sheet iron,
jeans, a jewel-eyed
alabaster goat. Is that
why I'm here? Everyone
needs kudos, from newborns
to saviors. Nora, nearly three,
draws sunlight in golden bars,
not unlike an Impressionist painter.
I like to think of light this way,
dispensed in attaché cases
to illuminate as needed.
The famous poet said *write*
by the light of your wounds.
A drunk flies over his bicycle handlebars,
crumples by the side of the road.
Performed pain is still pain.
Some people born before the Model T
lived to see man walk on the moon.
To be strapped like that
to the masthead of history
would make me frantic.
At parties I'd shout
I'm frantic, and you? Like a fire,
hungry and resisting containment,
I'd pound at the windows, my
mouth full of hors d'oeuvres.
Outside—sweeping plains
of green flora and service stations.
Odd, for an apocalypse
to announce itself with such bounty.
I hear crickets chirp and think

of my weaker heart, the tiny one
sewn behind the one
that beats. It lives there
made entirely of watery pink light,
flapping at dawn like a baby's cheek.
It doesn't take much
to love a saint like me.
On a gravel road, the soft tissues
of my eye detect a snake curling
around a tree branch. Because I am here
each of these things has a name.

A BOY STEPS INTO THE WATER

and of course he's beautiful
goosebumps over his ribs
like tiny fists under a thin sheet   the sheet
all mudwet and taste of walnut

and of course I'm afraid of him
of the way keeping him a secret will make him
inevitable   I will do anything to avoid
getting carried away   sleep nightly with coins

over my eyes   set fire to an entire
zodiac   mecca is a moth
chewing holes in a shirt I left
at a lover's house   a body loudly

consumes days and awaits the slow
fibrillation of its heart   a lightning rod
sits in silence until finally   the storm
now the boy is scooping up minnows

and swallowing them like a heron
I'm done trying to make sense
of any of this   no one will believe anything
that comes out a mouth like mine

WAKE ME UP WHEN IT'S MY BIRTHDAY

Brow-wrinkling beloveds—shhhh.
      What I do to my body is nobody's
business. Practice ignoring whatever
      you're able: the names I forget,
my mistimed erections, teeth marks I leave
      in your gold. It's amazing what you can find
if you just dissect everything. Once
      I pulled a glowing crystal from my beard
and buried it in the earth. The next day
      I went to the spot and dug up a silver trumpet
I still haven't learned to play. Jealousy,

      sexual or otherwise, begins with touch—
tears fall on a stone and the stone suddenly
      wants eyes; a countess is fished from the ocean
and her pearls slip quiet into the captain's
      pocket. Take it all out on me. Or, take it up
with my maker, who is right now
      stiff with guilt sitting in heaven, chain-
chewing whitening gum. In the first
      language, the word for *bridge* translates
to *death by water*. The iron law of congestion:
      traffic expands to flood any available

space. Keep a soul open and it's bound
      to fill up with scum. It's all I can do to quiver
in and out of my jeans each day, to keep
      my fingers out of the wrong mouths.
A man creates the most joy in the abstract,
      when you can remove his actual body,

its shear carapace and bleeding gums. Cut it
        away, the entire boring envelope, and marvel
at what remains: a pulsing vacuum bag
        stuffed with rubies and bone spurs, a pink
lighthouse only barely heavier than its light.

II. HUNGER

"The evidence of a successful miracle is the return of hunger."
—FANNY HOWE

WHAT SEEMS LIKE JOY

how much history is enough history   before we can agree
to flee our daycares   to wash everything away and start over
leaving laptops to be lost in the wet along with housecats and Christ's
own mother   even a lobster climbs away from its shell a few
times a life   but every time I open my eyes I find
I am still inside myself   each epiphany dull and familiar
oh now I am barefoot   oh now I am lighting the wrong end
of a cigarette   I just want to be shaken new like a flag whipping
away its dust   want to pull out each of my teeth
and replace them with jewels   I'm told what seems like joy
is often joy   that the soul lives in the throat plinking
like a copper bell   I've been so young for so many years
it's all starting to jumble together   joy jeweling copper
its plink   a throat   sometimes I feel beautiful and near dying
like a feather on an arrow shot through a neck   other times
I feel tasked only with my own soreness   like a scab on the roof
of a mouth   my father believed in gardens   delighting
at burying each thing in its potential for growth   some years
the soil was so hard the water seeped down slower than the green
seeped up   still he'd say *if you're not happy in your own yard*
you won't be happy anywhere   I've never had a yard but I've had apartments
where water pipes burst above my head   where I've scrubbed
a lover's blood from the kitchen tile   such cleaning
takes so much time you expect there to be confetti at the end
what we'll need in the next life   toothpaste   party hats
and animal bones   every day people charge out of this world
squealing   good-bye human behavior!   so long acres
of germless chrome!   it seems gaudy for them to be so cavalier
with their bliss   while I'm still here lurching into my labor
hanging by my hair from the roof of a chapel   churchlight thickening
around me   or wandering into the woods to pull apart eggshells   emptying
them in the dirt   then sewing them back together to dry in the sun

BEST SHADOWS

You love when I'm like this, coated
with ranch dressing and rum. Look under

the bandages—an entire saint! Here's
what I own: a blackened coin and yes

for an answer. The countdown to the next major miracle
is on. Till then, I'll manage less and less. Did you rejoice

when you left? If you spin around quickly enough,
it's almost like being drunk. This has to do

with the liquids in your skull. I never told you
about the tiny beetle I saw crawl out of your ear, afraid

you wouldn't sleep in my bed again if you knew.
I wish you were here so I could bend a mirror

around your face, pour you back into you. Ah,
there goes another wish. Minute to minute I'm fine—

right lung, left lung, blink—but the late hours
get so long. One of the best shadows I cast is the one

that ripples over water. There is so much ink
in our river now; it's swallowing up all the green.

Do you know how hard it is to dig a new river?
To be the single tongue in a sack full of teeth?

Sometimes I get the feeling you're never coming back.

PORTRAIT OF THE ALCOHOLIC WITH MOTHS AND RIVER

some moths don't even have mouthparts using
only stored caterpillar energy
their lives are measured in days scissoring
tributaries   for every you there
are a hundred moths luxuriously
dying their spirits spoiled by excess

what you lack and the punishment for your
lacking are the same   paling tulips gray-
ing fingernails   a body nearly stops
then doesn't I have seen it a man slips
beneath a blanket emerges clutching
himself saying this is mine I found it

rivers often do the same thing claiming
whatever they pour into   cathedrals
gardens snakeholes do you see how afraid
I am for you   all men are drawn to the
black water moonless the quiet drums a
name it's not yours it's not mine listen

to make life first you need a dying star
this seems important with you so close to
collapsing yourself   the mute swan's final
burst of song   I know you've tried this before
when they asked where it hurt you motioned in
a circle to the ground under your feet

RIMROCK

Without the benefit of fantasy
I can't promise I'll be of any use.

Left to the real world I tend
to swell up like roots in the rain,

tend to get all lost in hymns
and astrology charts. Lately

I've been steaming away, thin
as cigarette paper, cleaning up

the squirrels that keep dying in my yard.
Each cascade of fur feels like a little tuft

of my own death. Am I being dramatic?
Mostly I want to be letters—not

their sounds, but their shapes
on a page. It must be exhilarating

to be a symbol for everything at once:
the bone caught in a child's windpipe,

the venom hiding in a snake's jaw.
I used to be so afraid of nature.

Peering up at a rush of rimrock
I imagined how unashamed it would be

to crush even me, a tiny stuttering boy
with glasses. I pictured myself

reduced to a warm globe of blood
and yearned to become sturdy in my end-

lessness, to grow heavy and terrible
as molten iron poured down a throat. Still,

I don't know the rules. If I go looking
for grace and find it, what will grace

yield? Broken ribs, probably, flakes
of rust, an X marked in an atlas which itself

has been lost for ages. Oh, but I do
know what I am: moonstruck, stiff

as wet bamboo. I remember someone
once sang here, once strung together

a garland of near-holy moments.
It's serious business, this living.

As long as the earth continues
its stony breathing, I will breathe.

When it stops, I will shatter back
into gravity. Into quartz.

PRAYER

again I am thinking of self-love   filled with self-love   the stomach
of the girl who ate only hair was filled with hair   they cut
it out when she died   it formed a mold of her stomach   reducing
a life to its most grotesque artifact   my gurgling internal devotion
to myself   a jaw half-formed   there are words
I will not say   the muscle of my face smeared
with clay   I am more than the worry I make   I choose
my words carefully   we now know some angels are more terrifying
than others   our enemies are replaceable   the stones behind their teeth
glow in moonlight   compared to even a small star
the moon is tiny   it is not God but the flower behind God I treasure

BESIDES, LITTLE GOAT, YOU CAN'T JUST GO ASKING FOR MERCY

Besides, little goat, you can't just go asking for mercy.
With a body like that, it's easy to forget

about the spirit—the sun unfolding over your coat, your throat
too elegant for prayer. I like it fine, this daily struggle

to not die, to not drink or smoke or snort anything
that might return me to combustibility. Historical problem:

it's harder than you'd think to burn even what's flammable.
Once, I charged into your body and invented breath. Or,

I stumbled into your mouth and found you breathing. When I left,
I left a lozenge of molten ore on your tongue. Stony grain-pounder,

sleepy pattern-locator, do this: cover your wings, trust
the earth, spread your genes. Nothing here is owned. The ladder

you're looking for starts not on the ground but several feet below it.

THIRSTINESS IS NOT EQUAL DIVISION

I swear to God   I swear at God   I won't
mention what He does to me   I lack nothing I need
unless you count everything I want   I'm meant
to be spreading tenderness over the earth like seeds
like worms   instead I've been shoveling coal
into burning houses   fanning the ash   hold your
applause   hold the horns curling out from my skull
which are getting so long now and so sharp   if you think
of evolution as ancestral advice   then a baby's eyelids
drooping from fruitsugar could mean this world
is too sweet to bear awake   give me an orgy of sleep
give me sleep from every angle   for years I stood
in the semeny ginko staring at my hands   believing
in afterlives   thinking one day I'd wake into
a new kind of body   like a fish suddenly
breathing air through its eyes   it's easy to give life
as a gift   pull a fisherman from frozen water or
put a puppy in a Christmas box   but it's harder
to remember stillness is also a prize   consider
the composer's fever and the aria it delivered
or the beggar who woke to find a jewel
in his palm   once I saw a girl's death mask smoothed
by the kisses her father gave it nightly   once
I cut open my thigh on a razor wire fence and filled
the wound with Kleenex   somehow it healed leaving
only a long white scar   the penalties for my disregard
have always been oversoft   deterring nothing
I've made it clear I am not to be trusted with a body
always leaving mine bloodless as ice   with just a needle
of breath left in its lungs   sometimes when I run
I run like a beautiful man   in straight lines clean
as spidersilk   sometimes if I'm silent for long enough
even the wild around me stops moving

LONG PIG

I came to speak about luck but I fear dismantling what is already
simple so I will say only that if you are fortunate enough to have
a body you shouldn't leave it lying wet on the floor where anyone
could shred it to bits it is worth treating well   see also the perfect
pine replica of my breastbone which fell off the wall shattering across
the tile   see also the sixteen-celled fetus half-mine lost in the plumbing
of an apartment we lovingly called the Trash Castle   say something or say
nothing the options are always the same and often so are the results

some birds have feathers but can't fly and even they cherish
their flesh bathing it in sand or snow   every animal longs to be bare
to chew through its fur and melt directly into weather like dry ice   there is
a moment of startle when a thing really sees itself for the first time
a shock of *hey me it's me you* in this way we are all each other's mascots
equal and opposite   in my dreams I am a cannibal eating long pig
in a strange unmappable country   it seeps into my living I stay a throb
of hunger and brainstem if you move even a little I will take you in my mouth

BEING IN THIS WORLD MAKES ME FEEL LIKE
A TIME TRAVELER

visiting a past self. Being anywhere makes me thirsty.
When I wake, I ask God to slide into my head quickly before I do.
As a boy, I spit a peach pit onto my father's prayer rug and immediately

it turned into a locust. Its charge: devour the vast fields of my ignorance.
The Prophet Muhammad described a full stomach as containing
one-third food, one-third liquid, and one-third air.

For years, I kept a two-fists-long beard and opened my mouth only to push air out.
One day I stopped in a lobby for cocktails and hors d'oeuvres
and ever since, the life of this world has seemed still. Every night,

the moon unpeels itself without affectation. It's exhausting, remaining
humble amidst the vicissitudes of fortune. It's difficult
to be anything at all with the whole world right here for the having.

AGAINST DYING

if the body is just a parable
about the body if breath
is a leash to hold the mind
then staying alive should be
easier than it is most sick
things become dead things
at twenty-four my liver was
already covered in fatty
rot my mother filled a tiny
coffin with picture frames
I spent the year drinking
from test tubes weeping
wherever I went somehow
it happened wellness crept
into me like a roach nibbling
through an eardrum for
a time the half minutes
of fire in my brainstem
made me want to pull out
my spine but even those
have become bearable so
how shall I live now
in the unexpected present
I spent so long in a lover's
quarrel with my flesh
the peace seems over-
cautious too-polite I say
stop being cold or *make*
that blue bluer and it does
we speak to each other
in this code where every word
means *obey* I sit under
a poplar tree with a thermos

of chamomile feeling
useless as an oath against
dying I put a sugar cube
on my tongue and
swallow it like a pill

PORTRAIT OF THE ALCOHOLIC WITH RELAPSE FANTASY

You're in a car and crying and amazed
at how bad it feels to do bad things. Then

you're in a hotel bathroom with blood
on your undershirt and the smell of a too-

chlorinated pool outside. You know
one hundred ways to pray to the gods

rippling beneath that water. Confess, tangle,
pass through. Once your room is dark

they come inside, dripping wet. When you show
them the burnt place on your arm,

they show you the bands of flesh cut
from their thighs. You suck their tongues,

trace the blisters under their wings. It's so lucky,
this living forever all at once. When you turn

on the lights, you're inconsolably
glad. You could stop this whenever, but why?

ORCHIDS ARE SPROUTING FROM THE FLOORBOARDS

Orchids are sprouting from the floorboards.
Orchids are gushing out from the faucets.
The cat mews orchids from his mouth.
His whiskers are also orchids.
The grass is sprouting orchids.
It is becoming mostly orchids.
The trees are filled with orchids.
The tire swing is twirling with orchids.
The sunlight on the wet cement is a white orchid.
The car's tires leave a trail of orchids.
A bouquet of orchids lifts from its tailpipe.
Teenagers are texting each other pictures
of orchids on their phones, which are also orchids.
Old men in orchid penny loafers
furiously trade orchids.
Mothers fill bottles with warm orchids
to feed their infants, who are orchids themselves.
Their coos are a kind of orchid.
The clouds are all orchids.
They are raining orchids.
The walls are all orchids,
the teapot is an orchid,
the blank easel is an orchid,
and this cold is an orchid. Oh,
Lydia, we miss you terribly.

THE NEW WORLD

Do I have to talk about fear?
So much has already been said
about hidden spiders, compass needles
lodged in the soft of an eye.

> The soul is a thirsty
> antelope nervously lapping up
> water from a pool
> in the hunter's backyard.

Or so I've been told. Sometimes
when I listen to old Persian music
I get so sad I can actually smell rosewater.
This is a Real Thing That Happens.

> If home is the question,
> the honest answers must all be elegant
> forgeries. Must be sprinkled
> with sumac. Droughts occur

constantly under God's holy watch.
His response? He yawns
immortally on his throne,
fans himself with an elephant ear.

> *The lion was so exhausted and numb*
> *that a person might've thought*
> *they could*
> *kiss it.*

The calculus of desperation yields
everything in miniature. I fell in love

with the volume of an earlobe
rotated around the axis of a spine.

My dear,
how did you
end up
like this?

Withhold the accident. Withhold
the tiny aches. Withhold the body's
capacity for desiccation, for ineffable
grief. There are no new worlds left to dream.

There is no new world.

AGAINST HELL

With sensitive enough instruments even uprooting a shrub
         becomes a seismic event. So much of living is about understanding
scale—a tiny crystal dropped in a river turns the entire river

            red. The hands that folded me into my body were not punishing me
        nor could they ever be punished, while the hands of the idol sculptor
           were cut off and tossed to the dogs. This is proof of something,

but what? Maybe that retribution has grown vulgar, with sin now
        inevitable as summer sweat. Most days I try hard to act human, to breathe
like a human and speak with the same flat language, but often

          my kindness is clumsy—I stop a stranger to tie his shoe and
      end up kissing his knees. I believe in luck and am barely troubled
         by its volatility. I remember too well the knife held to my gut, the beehive

I once spat at for hours without getting stung. The charm of this
        particular dilemma: faith begins where knowing ends. The undertaker
spills his midday latte on a corpse, a chariot wheel flies off

         and kills a slave, and nobody asks for a refund. The unexpected
      happens, then what? The next thing. I feel most like a person when
        I am forcing something to be silent, holding a rat underwater or twining

shut the jaw of a lamb before it's roasted on the spit. It's only natural to smell
        smoke and feel hungry, to lean into the confusion of tongues. If I am
to be punished for any of this, it will be thousands of years too late.

PALMYRA

after Khaled al-Asaad

bonepole bonepole since you died
there's been dying everywhere
do you see it slivered where you are
between a crown and a tongue   the question still
more god or less   I am all tangled
in the smoke you left   the swampy herbs
the paper crows   horror leans in and brings
its own light   this life so often inadequately
lit   your skin peels away   your bones soften
your rich unbecoming   a kind of apology

when you were alive your cheekbones
dropped shadows across your jaw   I saw a picture
I want to dive into that darkness   smell
the rosewater   the sand   irreplaceable
jewel how much of the map did you leave
unfinished   there were so many spiders
your mouth a moonless system
of caves filling with dust
the dust thickened to tar
your mouth opened and tar spilled out

UNBURNABLE THE COLD IS FLOODING OUR LIVES

the prophets are alive but unrecognizable to us
as calligraphy to a mouse   for a time they dragged

long oar strokes across the sky   now they sit
in graveyards drinking coffee forking soapy cottage cheese

into their mouths   my hungry is different than their hungry
I envy their discipline but not enough to do anything about it

I blame my culture   I blame everyone but myself
intent arrives like a call to prayer and is as easy to dismiss

Rumi said the two most important things in life were beauty
and bewilderment   this is likely a mistranslation

after thirty years in America my father now dreams in English
says he misses the dead relatives he used to be able to visit in sleep

how many times are you allowed to lose the same beloveds
before you stop believing they're gone

some migrant birds build their nests over rivers
to push them into the water when they leave   this seems

almost warm   a good harm   the addictions
that were killing me fastest were the ones I loved best

turning the chisel toward myself I found my body
was still the size of my body   still unarmored as wet bread

one way to live a life is to spend each moment asking
forgiveness for the last   it seems to me the significance

of remorse would deflate with each performance   better
to sink a little into the earth and quietly watch life unfold

violent as a bullring   the carpenter's house will always be
the last to be built   sometimes a mind is ready to leave

the world before its body   sometimes paradise happens
too early and leaves us shuddering in its wake

I am glad I still exist   glad for cats and moss
and Turkish indigo   and yet   to be light upon the earth

to be steel bent around an endless black   to once again
be God's own tuning fork   and yet   and yet

PORTRAIT OF THE ALCOHOLIC FROZEN IN BLOCK OF ICE

for Max

what we mean when we say immortal   bruised
    and bluefleshed   loathsome as glass pulled
from a child's mouth   of course freezing is terrible

        but what's worse is this silence   everything quiet
    as a bowl of fruit hardening under lava   sometimes
        I think about my father's farm   sizzling and biosecure

his ten thousand ducks all laying dead white eggs   for
    fun I imagine their beaks tugging out my hair   carrying away
each tuft to soften their tiny beds   years ago I would blow

        empty winebags up into pillows   combing
    baby powder through my hair I hiccupped
        through the night and in the morning I drank milk

to vomit myself well   what was it the skinny
    boy said as he shuffled politely off the gangplank?
something something   adore me to sleep   it's a long drive

        into manhood but such a short walk out   I spent so long
    shocking myself with my own carelessness   misnaming
        lovers and tripping over the homeless   until finally

the world crushed me to ice   the way a fever crushes you
    to sleep   a body transacts then expires   ghoulish
as a raven's foot   heavy and wet as rained-on fur   dear single-

        breasted archer of my dreams I heartily endorse your grief!
    it's hard to remember your ribs connect to your backbone
        until the chill in your chest reaches around for your spine

NEITHER NOW NOR NEVER

None of my friends want to talk
about heaven. How there is this eternity
and the one for those
more clerical with their faith.
I spend hours each week
saying *I can't hear you*
into a phone and courting the affections
of neighborhood cats, yet
somehow never find time to burn the thigh
of an ox or a stack of twenties. Thought,

penetrate my cloud of unknowing.
I remain a hungry child
and the idea of a land flowing with milk
and honey makes me excited,
but I do wonder what gets left out—
least favorite songs on favorite albums,
an uncle's conquered metastasis,
or the girl whose climaxes gave way to panic,
whose sobs awakened the feeling of prayer in me.
May they be there too, O Lord.
With each second passing over me
may that heaven grow and grow.

EVERYTHING THAT MOVES IS ALIVE AND A
THREAT—A REMINDER

Everything that moves is alive and a threat—a reminder
to be as still as possible. Devastation occurs

whether we're paying attention or not. The options: repair
a world or build a new one. Like the belled cat's

frustrated hunt, my offer to improve myself
was ruined by the sound it made. How do I look today,

better or worse than a medium-priced edible
arrangement? I am sealing all my faults with platinum

so they'll gleam like the barrel of a laser gun. Astronomy: the luminosity
of Venus reminds me to wear orange in the woods. Nobody

ever pays me enough attention. I've spent my whole adult life
in a country where only my parents can pronounce my name.

Please, spare me your attempts; I'm a victim of my own
invention. The desire to help others is a kind of symmetry,

an eccentricity of our species like blushing, gold teeth, and life
after children. I don't worry myself with what my doctor said

before he burst into flames. I just eat his wet blue pills,
stay emotionless as a fig. Muscle memory: a heart

calls for you by name. Come to bed with me, you honest thing—
let's break into science. I'll pluck you from my mouth

like an apple seed, weep with you over other people's lost pets.
The strangeness between us opens like a pinhole on the ocean floor:

in floods a fishing boat, a Chinese seabird, an entire galaxy
of starfish. We are learning so much so quickly. The sun

is dying. The atom is reducible. The god-harnesses
we thought we came with were just our tiny lungs.

WHAT USE IS KNOWING ANYTHING IF NO ONE IS AROUND

What use is knowing anything if no one is around
to watch you know it? Plants reinvent sugar daily
and hardly anyone applauds. Once as a boy I sat
in a corner covering my ears, singing Qur'anic verse

after Qur'anic verse. Each syllable was perfect, but only
the lonely rumble in my head gave praise. This is why
we put mirrors in birdcages, why we turn on lamps

to double our shadows. I love my body more
than other bodies. When I sleep next to a man, he becomes
an extension of my own brilliance. Or rather, he becomes
an echo of my own anticlimax. I was delivered

from dying like a gift card sent in lieu of a pound
of flesh. My escape was mundane, voidable. Now
I feed faith to faith, suffer human noise, complain
about this or that heartache. The spirit lives in between

the parts of a name. It is vulnerable only to silence
and forgetting. I am vulnerable to hammers, fire,
and any number of poisons. The dream, then: to erupt
into a sturdier form, like a wild lotus bursting into

its tantrum of blades. There has always been a swarm
of hungry ghosts orbiting my body—even now,
I can feel them plotting in their luminous diamonds

of fog, each eying a rib or a thighbone. They are
arranging their plans like worms preparing
to rise through the soil. They are ready to die
with their kind, dry and stiff above the wet earth.

NO IS A COMPLETE SENTENCE

The body happens
and we consequence up.

When I said I'd eat even
your baby fat, what I meant

was collect your meat
and deliver it to me, I'm tired

of chewing the same bones
day in and day out. Look me

in the eyes and stop being sad—
they just discovered the skull

of a mammoth in a pumpkin patch
a few miles from here.

As a boy I had a filling punched
out of my mouth. I found it

the next day in a tuft of onion grass
and tried to bite it back into my tooth.

The mammoth was a dumb beast,
all low forehead and too-close

eyes. The real world doesn't care
about our spiritual conditions,

just asks that we be well
enough to smile at its clamor.

What can I do for you,
little vermin? Little casket

of gold? Milk splashes
into a bowl and coronates

itself with a crown of droplets.
I too have been trying to exalt

my own body, but there is no switch
to flip for this. I fumble toward grace

like a vine searching for a wall.
Any drunk can tell you willpower's

useless, but that doesn't stop us
from trusting it—the drowning

man surfaces three times
before sinking completely. Are you

going to finish that tongue, my love?
I'll chew it up for you, spit it

down your throat. No blame
lies with the weak, with the steam

curling off the pot of hemlock
tea. God can always see us,

but he can especially see us now. You owe
me nothing anymore, you still-

twitching vein pulled from a neck,
you wiseblood, you wise new blood.

III. IRONS

" If love were in the flesh I would burn it out with hot irons
and be at peace."

—KAHLIL GIBRAN

PORTRAIT OF THE ALCOHOLIC FLOATING IN SPACE
WITH SEVERED UMBILICUS

in Fort Wayne I *drank the seniors*   Old Milwaukee
Old Crow   in Indianapolis I stopped   now I regret
every drink I never took   all around   coffee grounds
and eggshells   this sweating   a mouthful
of lime   as a boy I stole a mint green bra
from a laundromat   I took it home to try on
while my parents slept   filled its cups with the smallest
turnips in our pantry   the underwire grew
into me like a strangler fig   my blood roiled then
as now   back on earth frogspit is dripping
down wild aloe spikes   salmon are bullying
their way upstream   there is a pond I leapt into once
with a lonely blonde boy   when we scampered out one of us
was in love   I could not be held responsible
for desire   he could not be held at all   I wonder
where he is now   if he looked up he might see
me   a sparkling   I always hoped that when I died
I would know why   my brother will be so sad   he will tell
his daughter I was better than I was   he will leave out
my crueldrunk nights   the wet mattresses   my driving alone
into cornfields unsure whether I'd drive out   I wish
he were here now   he could be here   this cave
is big enough for everyone   look at all the diamonds

AN APOLOGY

Lord, I meant to be helpless, sex-
less as a comma, quiet as
cotton floating on a pond. Instead,
I charged into desire like a
tiger sprinting off the edge of
the world. My ancestors shot bones
out of cannons and built homes where
they landed. This is to say, I
was born the king of nothing, pulled
out from nothing like a carrot
slipped from soil. I am still learning
the local law: don't hurt something
that can smile, don't hold any grief
except your own. My first time—brown
arms, purple lips, lush as a gun—
we slumped into each others' thighs.
She said *duset daram, mano*
tanha bezar—I love you, leave
me alone. See? There I go scab-
picking again. You should just hang
me in a museum. I'll pose
as a nasty historical
fact, wave at cameras, lecture
only in the rhetoric of
a victim. As a boy I tore out
the one hundred and nine pages
about Hell in my first Qur'an.
Bountiful bloomscattering Lord,
I could feel you behind my eyes
and under my tongue, shocking me
nightly like an old battery.
What did I need with Hell? Now that
I've sucked you wrinkly like a thumb,

I can barely be bothered to
check in. Will I ever even know
when my work is done? I'm almost
ready to show you the mess I've made.

THE STRAW IS TOO LONG, THE AXE IS TOO DULL

a skull floats up from the pond and makes a sound like a gull
      shriek to warn me I have stood here too long   when it dies
back into the water it leaves silence all around and reedstems

        like boiled femurs leaning away   such provocation
    is needed to pull a man open to expose his earthmeat
anyone can understand a skull even the seeds in my pocket

are cracking awake   I can feel the long scar around my neck
     glowing the dock underneath my feet
melting into rust   god in his inestimable wisdom is on the side

       of the big battalions   instead of my one gashable body he would
    have preferred fifty   now my shoes are soaking through
      now the math seems obvious   blue water plus yellow sun equals

green plants it's almost too simple to speak   I am inconsolable I need
     pondfoam and boxed wine in a coffee mug or soothing
saffron and bay leaves I need to be poured dry instead of this slow

      seeping   it hurts to even think about the leak in my brain
   where brackish water trickles in and memory trickles out
      with what do I mend a hole like that   answer me   with what

MY KINGDOM FOR A MURMUR OF FANFARE

It's common to live properly, to pretend
        you don't feel heat or grief: wave nightly

at Miss Fugue and Mister Goggles before diving
        into your nightcap, before reading yourself

a bedtime story or watching your beloved sink
        to the bottom of a lake and noting his absence

in your log. The next day you drop his clothes off
        at Goodwill like a sack of mail from a warplane

then hobble back to your hovel like a knight moving
        only in L's. It is comfortable to be alive this way,

especially now, but it makes you so vulnerable to shock—
        you ignore the mortgage and find a falconer's glove

in your yard, whole hand still inside. Or you arrive home
        after a long day to discover your children have grown

suddenly hideous and unlovable. What I'm trying
        to say is I think it's okay to accelerate around

corners, to grunt back at the mailman and swallow all
        your laundry quarters. So much of everything is dumb

baffle: water puts out fire, my diseases can become
        your diseases, and two hounds will fight over a feather

because feathers are strange. All I want is to finally
          take off my cowboy hat and show you my jeweled

horns. If we slow dance I will ask you not to tug
          on them, but secretly I will want that very much.

EVERY DRUNK WANTS TO DIE SOBER IT'S HOW WE BEAT THE GAME

Hazrat Ali son-in-law of the prophet was martyred by a poisoned sword
while saying his evening prayers his final words *I am successful*   I am
successful I want to carve it in my forehead I've been cut into before
it barely hurt I found my body to be hard and bloodless as
glass still for effect I tore my shirt to tourniquets   let me now be
calm for one fucking second let me be open to revision eternity looms
in the corner like a home invader saying *don't mind me I'm just here to watch you nap*
if you throw prayer beads at a ghost they will cut through him soft
as a sabre through silk   I finally have answers to the questions I taught
my mother not to ask but now she won't ask them   as a child I was so tiny
and sweet she would tuck me in saying *moosh bokhoradet* a mouse
should eat you I melted away that sweet like sugar in water like once-fresh
honey dripping down a thigh   today I lean on habit and rarely unstrap
my muzzle it's hard to speak of something so gauche as ambition
while the whole wheezing mosaic chips away but let it be known
I do hope one day to be free of this body's dry wood   if living proves
anything it's that such astonishment is possible   the kite loosed
from its string outpaces its shadow an olive tree explodes
into the sky dazzling even the night   I don't understand the words
I babble in home movies from Tehran but I assume
they were lovely I have always been a tangle of tongue and pretty
want   in Islam there are prayers to return almost anything even
prayers to return faith I have been going through book after book pushing
the sounds through my teeth   I will keep making these noises
as long as deemed necessary until there is nothing left of me to forgive

TASSIOPEIA

the rainwater here is full of phosphorous   if you drink too much
your kidneys fail   everything has limits   my grandfather fixed watches

for half a century until cataracts thick as figskin took his eyes   we tell
this kind of story to stay humble   consider the carnival geek choking

on chicken blood   consider the dazzling fortress of copper sucked back
into the earth   the soldiers tumbling into the split were bad seeds

they never did sprout   the best part of God is the math of God
you can count the pearls leading from here to him   sometimes

faith feels too far away to be of any use   a distant moon built
from the prophets' holy bones   other times it's so near

I can hold it between my teeth   I am as good as my word   which is to say
I'm keyless as the language of twins   the womb is a clammy pulp

of shredded tongues where we choose our obsessions   I came out
hot as a punched jaw   my head a beautiful blushing

pistachio   to reach me now you will have to figure out
my birthname   a hint   it rhymes with *Tassiopeia*

do you understand what I'm saying   I confess I have been trying
to seduce you   I'm not the fat egg I claimed to be   I'm sorry for that

and for all the tears   the delicate emotions should have felt more
hypothetical   I have mastered this grammar and little more

PORTRAIT OF THE ALCOHOLIC WITH CRAVING

I've lost the unspendable coin I wore around
      my neck that protected me from you, leaving it
bodyhot in the sheets of a tiny bed in Vermont. If you
      could be anything in the world

          you would. Just last week they found the glass eye
    of a saint buried in a mountain. I don't remember
      which saint or what mountain, only
    how they said the eye felt warm

in their palms. Do you like
      your new home, tucked
away between brainfolds? To hold you
      always seemed as unlikely

          as catching the wind in an envelope. Now
    you are loudest before bed, humming like a child
      put in a corner. I don't mind
    much; I have never been a strong sleeper, and often

the tune is halfway lovely. Besides, if I ask you to leave
      you won't. My hands love you more
than me, wanting only to feed you and feed you.
      Tonight I outrank them

          but wisely you have prepared for famine.
    I am trying to learn from all this.
          It was you who taught me that if a man
    stands in silence for long enough

eventually only the silence remains. Still,
        my desire to please you is absolute.
Remember the cold night we spent
        spinning on my lawn?

           I wore only basketball shorts
and a pair of broken sandals.
        I tied my hair back and
laid out a hammer, some rope,

a knife. What I was building was a church.
        You were the preacher and I the congregation,
and I the stage and I the cross and I the choir.
        I drank all the wine and we sang until morning.

FUGU

the liver of a blowfish is said to
be the tastiest part   it's also the
most toxic an ounce enough to kill ten
men   I have avoided it completely
which is not to say I've been unreckless
as a boy I saw a wolf in the shade

of a yew tree   I stared   it stared at my
staring   I whispered *banam-e-khudah*
it bolted   it could have shredded me like
a paper kite in a storm   I used to
believe my father's umbrella caused the
rain   he was so powerful   nobody
has turned out to be as powerful as
I believed my father to be   least of
all my father with his insulin and
heart medication   now he can't even
eat the fruit he grows which doesn't stop him
from growing it   he dries it sends boxes
of pressed quince apple cherry peach pear plum

that I struggle to love other men is
a lie I've uttered with confidence at
certain convenient moments in my life
I can't imagine anything less true
now with the dizzying sweet fruit still stuck
in my teeth   my gums and tongue tinted green
a quiet question answering itself

RIVER OF MILK

bear with me   it wasn't long ago I was brainless
lazily pulling fireflies into my teeth   chewing them

into pure light   so much of me then was nothing
I could have fit into a sugar cube   my body burned

like a barnful of feathers   nothing was on fire
but fire was on everything   the wild mustard

the rotting porch chair   a box of birth records   eventually
even scorched earth goes green   though beneath it

the dead might still luxuriate in their rage   my ancestor
was a dervish saint   said to control a thick river of dark milk

under his town   his people believed
he could have spared them a drought   they ripped him to pieces

like eagles tearing apart a snake   immediately they were filled
with remorse   instead of burying him   they buried a bag

of goat bones and azalea   my hair still carries that scent
my eyes   black milk and a snake's flicking tongue

does this confuse you   there are so many ways to be deceived
a butcher's thumb pressed into the scale   a strange blue dress

in a bathtub   the slowly lengthening night   I apologize
I never aimed at eloquence   I told my mother I wouldn't live

through the year   then waited for a disaster   sitting cheerfully
on cinder blocks pulled from a drained pond   tossing

peanuts to squirrels   this is not the story she tells   hers filled
with happy myths   fizzy pistons and plummy ghosts

it's true I suppose   you grow to love the creatures you create
some of them come out with pupils swirling   others with teeth

GOD

I am ready for you to come back. Whether in a train full of dying
        criminals or on the gleaming saddle of a locust, you are needed again.

The earth is a giant chessboard where the dark squares get all the rain.
        On this one the wet is driving people mad—the bankers all baying

in the woods while their markets fail, a florist chewing up flowers
        to spit mouthfuls here and there as his daughter's lungs seize shut

from the pollen. There is a flat logic to neglect. Sweet nothings sour
        in the air while the ocean hoots itself to sleep. I live on the skull

of a giant burning brain, the earth's core. Sometimes I can feel it pulsing
        through the dirt, though even this you ignore. The mind wants what it wants:

daily newspapers, snapping turtles, a pound of flesh. The work I've been doing
        is a kind of erasing. I dump my ashtray into a bucket of paint and coat myself

in the gray slick, rolling around on the carpets of rich strangers
        while they applaud and sip their scotch. A body can cause almost anything

to happen. Remember when you breathed through my mouth, your breath
        becoming mine? Remember when you sang for me and I fell to the floor,

turning into a thousand mice? Whatever it was we were practicing
        cannot happen without you. I thought I saw you last year, bark wrapped

around your thighs, lurching toward the shore at dawn. It was only mist
        and dumb want. They say even longing has its limits: in a bucket, an eel

will simply stop swimming long before it starves. Wounded wolves will pad
        away from their pack to die lonely and cold. Do you not know how scary

it can get here? The talons that dropped me left long scars around
my neck that still burn in the wind. I was promised epiphany, earth-

honey, and a flood of milk, but I will settle for anything that brings you now,
you still-hungry mongrel, you glut of bone, you, scentless as gold.

DESPITE THEIR SIZE CHILDREN ARE EASY TO REMEMBER THEY WATCH YOU

despite their size children are easy to remember they watch you
watching them   the square root of your gaze   don't forget
how hard it is being young mindless and spitting up blood
rolled out a doorless cage all iris no white estranged from sense
mirror neurons double the pain they see   here is what I have lost clean teeth
god's grammar olives cedar salt   temptation rarely warns you
a useful model unpredictable as an arrow through the spine
its flight path   its feathery hole   who among us hasn't wished to burst

from our bodies ripe berries crushed under a tongue   for some
to live well is easy   a flea leaps and is unshocked by its flight
for others it's harder and hardly seems worth doing   the better a life
the more sadness it leaves   I do only what comes naturally obey my gut
pray at takeoffs never landings   mostly I look forward to sleep
my body shelved hallucinating tangled wood almond
blossoms wind near a river that smells like river   it's lovely
because it's simple   just say yes and step into the consequence

WAYS TO HARM A THING

Throw scissors at it.
Fill it with straw
and set it on fire, or set it
off for the colonies with only
some books and dinner-
plates and a stuffed bear
named Friend Bear for me
to lose in New Jersey.
Did I say *me*? Things
have been getting
less and less hypothetical
since I unhitched myself
from your bedpost. Everyone
I love is too modern
to be caught
grieving. In order
to be consumed
first you need to be consumable,
but there is not a single
part of you I could fit
in my mouth. In a dream
I pull back your foreskin
and reveal a fat vase
stuffed with crow
feathers. This seems a faithful
translation of the real thing. Another
way to harm something is to
melt its fusebox,
make it learn to live
in the dark. I still want
to suck the bones out
from your hands,
plant them like the seeds

we found in an antique
textbook, though those
never sprouted and may not
have even been seeds.
When I was a sailor I found
a sunken ziggurat, spent
weeks diving through room
after room discovering
this or that sacred
shroud. One way to bury
something is to bury it
forever. When I was water
you poured me out
over the dirt.

PERSONAL INVENTORY: FEARLESS (TEMPORIS FILA)

*"I know scarcely one feature by which man can be distinguished from apes, if it be not
that all the apes have a gap between their fangs and their other teeth."*
—CAROLUS LINNÆUS

A gap, then,
a slot for fare.

I used my arms to learn *two*,
my fingers to learn *ten*.

My grandfather kept an atlas so old
there was a blank spot in the middle of Africa.

I knew a girl who knew every bird's Latin name.

I kissed her near a polluted river
and would have been fine
dying right there,

but nature makes no such jumps.
One thing,

then the next. America
is filled with wooden churches
in which I have never been baptized.

I try not to think of God as a debt to luck
but for years I consumed nothing
that did not harm me
and still I lived, witless

as a bird flying over state lines.

I would be more grateful
if being alive hadn't seemed so effortless,

the way I'd appreciate gravity more
if I'd had trouble floating in my teens.

Still, I apologize.

My straight white teeth have yellowed
and I can't tell a crow from a blackbird.

I'm sorry. I'm sorry.
This may be me at my best.

SO OFTEN THE BODY BECOMES A DISTRACTION

So often the body becomes a distraction—
delicate husk, inconvenient hair,
the bizarre need to recharge. I've heard
you die young if you don't sleep, but if you do
you'll just snooze through your extra time.
Like the headless grasshopper and his still-
twitching legs, I'm learning how much of myself
I don't actually need. It exists, a world without
this dumb neck. My whole form is mostly
skeleton and loose meat; that I've managed
anything at all seems cause for praise. Some say
there is life after the body, mysterious
as a tooth melting out an ice cube. A year ago
I blew the drugs out of my nose and immediately,
I was overwhelmed by the smell of semen
and gingerbread. Now I listen for the sighs
of people who love me, each agitation I create
a reminder that I am less than constant
in my grace. Will I ever be a great man? Will I
ever be one of the guys? Tarrc be tockmesh mire,
Kavehi be babash. The leek looks like its seed,
and little Kaveh looks like his father. See how
I am all rosejuice and wonderdrunk? See how
my throat is filling with salt? Boil me. Divide
me. Wrap me in paper and return me to earth. One day
I will crack open underneath the field mushrooms.
One day I will wake up in someone else's bones.

I WON'T LIE THIS PLAGUE OF GRATITUDE

I won't lie this plague of gratitude
   is hard to bear I was comfortable
in my native pessimism not this spun-
   sugar fantasy last night I made actual

      cake there were no worms in the flour no
   bloody whirls in the eggs afterwards the minor
      holiday below my waistband remained festive
   as ever when I touched two breasts each one

was my favorite not long ago I was hard to even
   hug like ribbons of cartilage cut
from a lamb I dressed in shredded roses
   and pistachio shells I drank an entire language

      and flung tar at whatever moved
   until the world cut me open like a tube of paint
      until it crushed me between its fingers
   like a hornet none of it was graceful

I had to learn to love people one at a time
   singing *hey diddle diddle will you suffer me*
a little how could they say no
   how could they say anything I kept

      biting their tongues I kept clicking
   my heels now I am cheery
      and Germanic like a drawer full
   of strudel I always wanted to be a saint

but I thought I'd be one of the miserable
       ones   sainted by pain   burnt alive inside
a brazen bull   instead I weep openly at obnoxious
       beauty   cello music comes in

           from blocks away and I lose it completely
     there is a word for these fits of incomprehensible
        delight   I said it last night
     when my mouth was full of cake

PORTRAIT OF THE ALCOHOLIC STRANDED ALONE ON A DESERT ISLAND

I live in the gulf
between what I've been given
and what I've received.

Each morning, I dig into the sand
and bury something I love.
Nothing decomposes.

It might sound ungrateful to say
I expected poetry, but I did—

palm forests and clouds above them
arranged like Dutch still lifes,
musically-colored fauna lounging
in perpetual near-smiles.

Instead, these tumors under the surf.

Wildness: to appear
where you are unexpected.

My favorite drugs are far from here.

Our father, who art in Heaven—always
just stepped out, while Earth,
the mother, everywheres around.

It all just means so intensely: bones
on the beach, calls from the bushes,
the scent of edible flowers
floating in from the horizon.

I hold my breath.

The boat I am building
will never be done.

Recent Titles from Alice James Books

Alice James Books has been publishing poetry since 1973. The press was founded in Boston, Massachusetts as a cooperative wherein authors performed the day-to-day undertakings of the press. This collaborative element remains viable even today, as authors who publish with the press are also invited to become members of the editorial board and participate in editorial decisions at the press. The editorial board selects manuscripts for publication via the press's annual, national competition, the Alice James Award. Alice James Books seeks to support women writers and was named for Alice James, sister to William and Henry, whose extraordinary gift for writing went unrecognized during her lifetime.

Designed by Mary Austin Speaker

Printed by McNaughton & Gunn